BETWEEN LOOKING

poems by

Virginia Barrett

Finishing Line Press
Georgetown, Kentucky

BETWEEN LOOKING

For my parents,
Jeannine Clark Dunlap and Jon Sherwood Barrett

ACKNOWLEDGMENTS

Annapurna Magazine: "After Separation the Kitchen Fills," "Appetites," "Breakfast
    with Flower in Small Vase"
Apple Valley Review: "Village Sketch"
Belle Rêve Literary Journal: "Rite of Passage—a Georgian Aesthetic"
Boned—a collection of skeletal writings: "Ritual"
Flatbush Review: "Mid-June," "Waking to Emily"
Forage: "Self-Portrait as the Landscape Painter in Italy"
Howl of the Wild Anthology (Winterwolf Press): "Forgetting"
Midnight Circus (EAB Publishing): "Spring: Break"
Narrative Magazine: "Hand-Wash" (excerpt from "Clothesline")
Panoply, A Literary Zine: "April Morning"
Pilgrimage: "On Love in the Royal BC Museum"
Raven Chronicles: "Still Life with Rain"
Riverbabble: "Black"
Roar: Literature and Revolution by Feminist People: "The Broken Pitcher"
Sabal (The Best of Eckerd College Writers' Conference): "Dusk," "Washerwoman
    Near Trouville"
The Birds We Piled Loosely: "Brimstone"
The Ekphrastic Review: "Rothko Contemplating Suicide"
The Fem: "Myth"
The Literary Nest: "The Birds Come Back Each Year," "The Repair"
The Machinery: "St. Petersburg [Florida] with Mandelstam"

Publisher: Leah Maines
Editor: Christen Kincaid
Cover Art: Ashley J. Benton. Detail from the painting *Reflecting*.
    www.ashleybentonstudio.com
Author Photo: Bobby Coleman
Cover Design: Leah Huete

Printed in the USA on acid-free paper.
Order online: www.finishinglinepress.com
        also available on amazon.com

Author inquiries and mail orders:
Finishing Line Press
P. O. Box 1626
Georgetown, Kentucky 40324
U. S. A.

Table of Contents

3 Star List

I shut my eyes in order to see.
Paul Gauguin

1

Intimations of a Self-Portrait

My Sight

after Vicente Aleixandre
for Janeen Armstrong

I was born one June night
amid contrast. Show me something: I am learning to see.
I was born. If we could only compose the longing
the twilight strokes with ease.
I was born. Our image rose wholly.
A vision under the sleeping flame, a fox.
Pushing, pushing. The city a crumpled map,
lines in the palm of the hand, a burning abstract.
Everything is now possible: the canvas stretched, the pigments crushed, the brush,
the infill of shapes without implication,
that roam like eyes or river pebbles,
like a blank orb that reflects
(look, look) in the altering light.

Brimstone

The fireflies go on with their brief beacons.
They felled the starlings' tree.

What did my grandmother say
before her lungs collapsed, tuckered out as a small
girl would be after *yonder* all day at the lake?

This was 1999 in the tiny kitchen.
She had the Bible beside her, dog-eared
and filled with paper placeholders marked
in her shaky hand.

Her fingers were ginger roots gnarled near
her face. They fluttered like spotted moths before
her eyes—the startling blue of them, alarmed with tears.

I want us together. I don't want
any of the family going to Hell . . .

                    there's fire down there!

I was looking more than listening. The peach left uneaten
on the forget-me-not plate. The refrigerator hum. I knew
she believed me damned.

When she died they said her lungs were black. She never
smoked a day in 92 years. Coal from her childhood
stove?

Fire down there . . . the drawn-out-Georgian-drawl,
the fear. There are times I hear
her voice still, how she complimented flowers flaming
with color; greeted like a neighbor, the Sun.

The azaleas spoke of debutante dresses,
gardenias compared the popular corsage.
Magnolias left their mess in the droning yard.

White

White glow of the mind,
of a crane or a god.
　　　　Homero Aridjis

morning overcast
white deer　　　under
a near-white sky

damp white daisies here and
here　　　　a bush full
of white star-shapes I can't name

the path through the forest
is marked by　　　　white paint on
the rough bark of trees

at night, owl is white
and the space in our
eyes　　　　through
which he flies

3

Washerwoman Near Trouville, c. 1872

*As to the "king of skies," I think I've already told you
that I consider Eugène Boudin to be my master.*
                                        Claude Monet

Clad in black all over—save a simple stroke
                of bright-bleached collar—
her one straight arm, anchored on the ground
as the other, bent and raised guides the hand to knead
and pound the cloth against the stone
the river will rinse clean.

On the rocks to her left, dashes of work
already done, draped in line spread out
to dry; by her gesturing arm are vivid touches—
a day's full travail for this woman who
                                works alone

were it not for the pearl-gray coat
                and celestial-blue dress
                of a figure to her right.
Seated on the sand, legs bent, arms folded
to hold her knees, she curls tight
                as if to keep herself from the chill of wind
                                urging distant sails.

A hat of woven straw hides her face, trimmed
with ribbon draped off the end
                of the sweeping, yellow brim.
The vast delight of gazing fixedly,
                or tangled with her thoughts?
                She watches the rippling
                reflections of a motionless space;
                                one that appears to move even so,
                                        given the grace
                                        of brush and tone—
                                        half the canvas a shifting sky.

Briefly we may wonder on whom,

or what she ponders, only we return

to the washerwoman:
small bent figure laboring under
a remarkable   immensity.

Endless chore!

See the dabs of paint listing toward
                    an imperceptible shore.

Last Picture
[*Portrait of Jeanne Hébuterne*]

after Amedeo Modigliani

She is long suffering
yet patient   the text says,

painted by him
with   "unmistakable warmth
and understanding"

She is plump with his child
her skirt   a blue swell
below a crossed wrap   carmine
full white sleeves

He will die soon of tubercular
meningitis   of alcohol
drugs

The day after his death
she will   throw herself
from a 5th floor window   leaving
their first child orphaned

Her eyes are light blue ovals
          no pupils
They see without   seeing
the blank sky to come

The narrowing   space

she will slip through

Virginia Creeper

for Kate Waller Barrett, 1857-1925
physician, humanitarian, and social reformer

They pulled me out with forceps as the full moon rose
over Manhattan in early June. Did anyone look at
the sky? I guard all the stories of who I was: a crying fit
because I wanted the Chitty Chitty Bang Bang car with
wings; sound asleep through detectives photographing

my mother in bed with another man. She claimed she
had to wake me as a baby to nurse—the Raggedy Ann
of my crib a mess of tatters now. I climbed to the top
of the chain link fence outside the church of my
preschool and wouldn't come down. The Vidalia
onion is sweet because of something in the soil. My
mother left twice . . . royal blue velvet beret . . .

Stepping outside she is free. I am my uncle throwing
furniture from a hotel window in Spain, kids blowing
peas out of straws that stuck in our hair—Ethan Allen
and his Green Mountain Boys. An executive grandfather
turned bibliophile married to a flapper who danced on
pianos at parties drunk until the doctor ordered
"quit!" First edition spines upright in a rotunda

inspired by Jefferson / the Pantheon in Rome. I will
not return to my father racked with tremors of delirium
in his bed upstairs. I loved the frozen meatloaf dinner
best. I woke up with the hollow in my belly and nowhere
to breathe. What lives deep inside the trees? Boil the sap
until almost gone to taste the syrup. Hide in the sugaring-
steam. A portrait of my great-great-grandmother

Kate at College of William and Mary I've never
seen. In Stafford County the wind took down the plantation
trees. But none of us live there now. A library in her honor
in the state of the name they gave this girl. The Algonquian
founded towns such as Werowocomoco; the Virginia
creeper with five leaflets turns deep red in fall.

Intimations of a Self-Portrait
[*Saint Catherine of Alexandria*]

after Barbara Longhi, 1552-1638

fixed gaze
             at us and the articulation of her hand
             near her heart—fingers loose like a brush—

images of
             female artists "rare as written
             references" why not paint yourself as a saint?

warm tones
             against black—light hair cascading into
             the folds of a noblewoman's clothes

her body
             discovered at Mount Sinai gave rise to a medieval
             cult—a stream of healing oil issuing from her pores

refusing to
             renounce her faith they beheaded
             her in the end

the wheel
             on which they intended to torture
             her burst at her touch

First Sleepover—Manhattan

up a flight of steps hard to reach no
elevator to take like where we

still lived without her
a narrow hall lit by a single

bulb the paint gray and a security
door clanky to unlock

so "no one bad" could get
in my mother said

but the bars invited hurt
because they were I thought

(the cage at the zoo where
lions stared . . .) and then

that night a ghostly screeching
rising up to her bedroom where

she slept soundly it seemed
while laid out like a little

corpse beside her there came
looming over me the moon

revealing fully nothing but
the raided chamber of treasured

rhymes *the cow jumped over*
or was it just a giant

dish of dreadful cream
keeping those wrenching

alley cats alive

Girlhood—Snow Angels

Just two trees with fire-leaves
seen for a moment through
the streetcar's window
at Church and 22nd are enough
to bring back the crispness,
the colors, the diving
into the raked piles, as if
diving would be the only
fall; falling into the death
and the coming white sleep
so cold, so cleanly impassive;
a beckoning to fall back
into the unforgiving give of
snow, the spreading and
un-spreading of legs /
arms—eyes gripped:
the immaculate sky

Portrait of Marguerite [1917-18]

after Amedeo Modigliani

The room is barely
indicated / She wears an unadorned dress of
mauve / Her body small-breasted, slim /
She looks over her shoulder at him / Face
elongated, thin

Her almond-eyes
stylized / Brown pupil-pools / White touch
of light / Narrow nose swooping down / Her
mouth outlined / Corners raised / Not quite
a smile / Tip of delicate chin

A second picture
survives / Same mauve dress but fully
frontal / "The artist gave her a strength of
character she may not have possessed"

They found cheap
lodgings in Montmartre / She eked out a
living like the rest / Her inner life lent to
him / Space suggested only by the
perspective of the chair

Old Barn—Autumn

> *The woolly bear caterpillar—with its 13*
> *distinct segments of black and reddish-brown—*
> *has the reputation of being able to forecast*
> *the coming winter weather.*
>
> The Old Farmer's Almanac

Struggling, I'd open the great
door to find them curled in

the threshold's deep groove, as
if it were the safe overwintering

cavity of a rock or log. I'd gather
them up, inspect their stripes

—bristly little creatures holding
themselves round and still in my

palm. I wanted their power
to divine: *The wider that middle*

brown section is, the milder
the coming winter will be. I learned

in spring they would turn into
tiger moths with the name, *Isabella,*

and fly away but for a time,
in the brisk air, they were

mine. Empty of livestock,
the old barn became a dark cavern,

imbued with its own lure
in the strong scent of hay.

Best Friend
[mill pond and moon]

in winter
the frozen mill
pond where we would skate
when our 4th grade teacher had the
time to shovel off the snow small and alone
we taught ourselves wobbly legs and bumps once
an older boy fell in but did not drown it was shallow
at the farther edge where we did not go he dried his socks
on the grate he placed over the fire lit in a rusted barrel with
holes laughing but he scared us all the same reckless he would
crash his car ten years later they buried him in the fall . . . the pond
was a kind of foreign body like the moon when full we were left to
wonder over in bladed tones escaping each our parents' drinking
keeping us separate but together awake with a weird agitated
glare ours but so removed a dense space of unknowing
underneath what cold bodies swam there once you
cut your wrist on a freak shard of ice but did not
die that time only the red on white and my
pale fascination after with the
lingering crescent-
shaped scar

The Broken Pitcher, 1891

after William-Adolphe Bouguereau

broken at her bare feet   one leg stretched
forward   big toe flexed

drew on a fashion

moist-earth eyes   her mouth   a pout
hair tied back   strands loosened to flax

for peasant imagery

a frayed shawl crossed   her slight chest
color of dried marigolds   white sleeves

investing it with

a skirt   over narrow hips   spread full
coarse cloth beaten clean   deep indigo

sexual allusion—

there is   an olive grove somewhere
near   a beloved tree   dark among fresh roses

the cracked pitcher

but she must sit   beside the village pump
raised knee   small hand held in the other

perhaps signifies lost

as if cupping something frail   like an egg
just found   a speckled shell

virginity or

beauty is what we walk toward   gazing
also concealed   how thirsty now

love abandoned

"What do you expect, you have to follow public
taste, and the public only buys what it likes. That's
why, with time, I changed my way of painting."

Village Sketch

Carol left after just six months but my neighbor had a mother.
Maple trees giving over to fire in the fall.
Salamanders in the heat mushed flat by tires.
Missy put the hood of her parka up, curled down by the cow.
The fleshy pink licked her like she was the calf taken to the lower barn.
I said I would never kiss with tongue.
Their big heads thrust through bars at milking time.
Lost languidness of fields.
Marble sidewalks laid from fragments we skipped over.
Wrecked boys stumbled around the old quarry down the road, night coming on.
They said old metal wedges embedded deep could impale you in the plunge.
I slipped once and hit my head tumbling knocked-out into the water.
The farmer's son put his hand up my shirt behind the church.
Missy conceived the child in the truck bed parked in their dirt driveway.
Cows lumbered back to the barn, swollen udders swaying.
The muted manure-drift of dusk, the shuddering leaves.

Rite of Passage—a Georgian Aesthetic

after Everett Hoagland

lip-smacking deep molasses buttery butter brown sugar crust
crusting eggs cracking whisking whisk wet bottom custard
candy gooey air wise-
                 woman
oven fun wide-sliced wonders we wide-eyed   big-breasted
bread rising huge love hugs bellies full sleepy belly-heads slow
southern heat
           and
plenty to eat firefly star twinkle night dreams
           NO BEDBUGS BITE

cooking for all us kids chirping birds of toss and tumble
nest learning to fly fly FLY   shoofly pie   pie   PIE
yummy tummies
           YONDER THERE

reels in time   fish in lake red mud body cake rite of passage dive
into the wake cousins cousins and kudzu twining all the trees
           WE   WE   WE
y'all teasin' me
water rhymes lap luscious all day play fat berries juicy
juice face stain watermelon seeds seeds seeds spitting slippery
high into the blaze-blue
                    sky
arch down buried bow earth waiting   watching head tossed
back laugh laughing   laugh
           BLESS OUR HEARTS

shoofly shoofly pie cry sweet summers child why you had to die
shoo shoo   fly

Clothesline

1. Hand-Wash

The woolens hung
       in early April—temperature

drop in the night—morning,
       she found them frozen solid.

My mother leaned them
       up against the wall; a row

of long-john legs and armed
       torsos behind the heavy Jøtul

made her laugh. Having
       burned all the furniture in the yard

my stepfather disappeared
       after the March thaw. We used boxes

for tables and chairs, draped
       them in old sheets. Just us now—our

first spring since her five-
       year absence—I was a reticent bird.

The wood stove gave
       off heat; the canary-yellow sweater she

knit while pregnant with me
       thawed first, collapsing on the floor.

2. Learning to Sew

Nearly thirteen, I began
to bleed. "Finally," she
said. An ending not a

beginning?—I learned
to wash my underwear
in the sink with cold

water, drape them to dry
on a thin line stretched
over the claw foot

tub. She taught me
how the needle pierced
the cloth doggedly

to coax an even seam.
Weighty old Singer
before me, I wondered

about birth, abandonment—
scowled to see, head bent
down. "Don't get so close,"

she warned, "That needle
could jam, fly right up
into your eye."

3. Yard Sale

     She strung a rope on the front
          porch for castoff
clothes, like folks who hung

     wash to dry (their underwear!)
          for all to see from
the road—our furniture haphazard

     on the grass. Everything bought from
          thrift stores, for sale
again; fifteen, I frowned,

     slouched as cars slowed down
          to browse, parked
quickly or accelerated—my

     mother leaving again. All day
          she ingratiated
herself to strangers, hand held

     out for coins and bills, "it all
          adds up in the end." Like
a model she wore a wide-

     brimmed hat, the price tag
          fluttering *pale moth, pale*
moth in the galling wind.

4. Making Vests

Fashioned from discounted slipcover
material, they hung
            from clothespins on a line

strung between trees in front of
the house where
            we lived with her third husband.

The coastal breeze moved the cloth
like bright sails;
            a handwritten sign stopped passersby—

I could barely sew enough of them
to keep stock.
            I needed money to pay my mother

rent but what I really wanted was
to write. Everything
            came out jumbled / the bin of

remnants I rummaged through
at the Five and Dime
            pairing fabrics for front and back. She

gave me the idea to create contrast—
match florals with stripes,
            paisleys with polka-dots: "the impact."

5. Ironing: Mimi's House

I followed
        her to the basement
        of the house

where she had lived
        as a girl, the ironing
        board in the boiler

room by the washing
        machine, lines strung
        between pipes

for drying, sheets
        hung like white shrouds—
        her mother

dying upstairs.
        The shoulder of the black
        blouse slipped

over the rounded
        end, "This is how
        Mother showed me

to smooth the inset
        of the sleeve," her voice
        deliberate as if

instructing a child
        [*Mommy and Mimi*
        don't speak

to each other]. Under
        the bare bulb
        I studied

my mother's
    hands—branched
    veins of age—

my own abiding
    silence
    pressed.

Ending with a Line by Euripides
[*Melpomene, the Muse of Tragedy*]

   after Elisabetta Sirani, 1638-1665

a turban wreathes her head
      sphere of silvery-blue
            abundant folds
                  strokes of
      black   hair trailing
            down

                  PROLOGUE

Melpomene means "to celebrate
with dance and song"
         but she became
               Tragedy's   inspiration

                  CHORUS

her gaze at us reflective—can a portrait
         of a muse   muse?
         a mask on the table   absence
         of eyes

                  SCENE

the artist died   suddenly
         at twenty-seven—a resplendent
         suffering—   grief,   lovesickness,
                              poisoning?

My web of woes is more complex by far.

2

On Dahlias and Mankind

Ode to a Jackhammer

My head's a womb, watery
chamber, blood pulsing through
an ocean cave. The inner
snail slips off to find another shell. Drum-
Drum-Drum. Sublime force of single-mindedness,
my Shiva-Shakti so heightened
I shut myself in the closet
to meditate. The body
a hollow husk—transcend—
your music in the ethereal
spheres! Hammer and chisel, mad
Camille Claudel could have used you to wreck
her sculptures not a silly sledgehammer—"mon cher,
Rodin, je te déteste." Michelangelo's Florentine
marble-man's hands are generous enough
for your job. *Whoever digs
a hole and scoops it out falls into the pit
they have made.* Studly lover
in the intrigue of contracts signed
behind closed doors; Casanova explosive air
exhaust! Great dildo of our urban drive,
supreme vibrator—which soon-to-be-deaf hunk
in a yellow helmet holds you today? Jack,
who brings the earth
to breathe. How I delight in my lime
green earplugs, kneaded
between my fingers; they rise
inside these quivering canals like inflatable rafts
moored in the sinking city of Throb.

Mid-June

I leave Goodwill with a book for
you. On Haight and Cole a guy sings

Cat Stevens, his old guitar plugged into
a small amplifier. I linger to catch

the chorus then walk toward the library
on Page to see if *Poetic Memory* is

waiting for me. It's after 3pm and
the wind is picking up. I can feel the fog

creep its way over the park as I could
always sense snow coming when I

was a girl. Vermont has nothing to say
to this West Coast weather—seasons so

vague they end up being one
continuous wave. A taste carried you

back four decades this morning eating
whitefish for breakfast. Grandma Gussie

offering you the same in Yiddish at her
Brooklyn table when you were a kid.

Two generations nearly gone. I mourned
my mother most in winter.

Waking to Emily

Rain on the roof after so much sun
not rain but heavy fog dripping in the drain outside

Drain outside   only sound
                 sound arousing   you
                                 somehow

                                 I drift off   dream again

         Your dress   at the top of the stairs
         a ghost dress   small and slim
                         floating   white
         the glass case   a coffin upright

Arranged as if being worn without a body
the intimate pocket   stitched at the hip to hold
paper and pencil should something come upon you

                                 Rapture perhaps

or only sound   of rain
                 a note for a poem
dripping its slow   slant-ache . . .

         Opening my eyes
                 to the rectangle of window
         the height of the old eucalyptus trees
                         in the Panhandle

Swaying slightly as you may have moved   composing
at the top of the stairs   *Morning's finest syllable*

Gray light of a daguerreotype

                 Your unattainable red hair

April Morning

The cost of flight is landing.
Jim Harrison

Six crows in the sky just when
Sunday tolls; must be an omen

of something. Roses galore
on the climbing vine—miraculous

having been barren last year. Nest
under the eaves of my art studio, they

come back each spring. Blue jay snaps
his sharp beak   *clack*   *clack*

at these juncos protecting their young.
Another year of paintbrushes and

wings. Birds are elusive abstractions.

Seeds & Twigs

When Merwin was a young man Pound sent him bits of
advice scribbled on postcards in pencil. Merwin called
these missives from his mentor "nuggets." At the time,
Pound was still locked up in the psycho ward of a D.C.
military hospital for ranting in favor of Mussolini; the plea
of insanity made by a Quaker lawyer saved him from being
shot. Merwin's favorite nugget said, "read seeds not twigs."
Many of the seeds I plant, in the open soil of the brick patio
outside this art studio I rent, rarely sprout. Rodents must
dig in the night and eat them. Other seeds do sprout, but six
months later; by that time I can't tell if they are something I
placed with intention, or a weed. [Walls confine this space
but seeds—and sirens—still penetrate.]

Any small twigs fallen on the patio birds have taken to
build their nests under the eaves near the bathroom I share
with a martial arts guy who's vegan, but never cleans the
toilet. Seems not killing animals doesn't pledge you to have
respect for humans—just like being credited as the force
behind radical shifts in modern English poetry doesn't
mean you're in your right mind. Pound backed Franco and
his Nationalist forces; where is Lorca's grave anyway?
"Impossible to imagine the poetry" wrote Merwin, "of
the whole Western world without him." Merwin meant
Lorca, not Pound but still, "read seeds" *is* an inspirational
metaphor from an early imagist. It's unexplainable, but
the largest twig on the patio—cut from the struggling
fuchsia bush—an unborn child used this morning to
engrave two lines in the stone sky. "I was sleeping in
peace. / Who bore into my dream?"

Spring: Break

Spring and all wrote Williams,
and all is all; fog breathes nothing,
if nothing comes to call. Her boat (it's crazy),
ascends through the sky; the clouds break—
to let it pass—birds don't fly.

Birds don't fly? She dreamed she grew
pale wings. Lorca gave us crickets,
now he could sing! Plath had a thing
for ovens—roasted heart; what we cook
in poems may tear us apart.

A paleo diet, his words taste good.
Gluten free—*to be, to be*—Hamlet
would. Hamlet would . . . NOT . . . now
give a dog a bone; we're comin' 'round
the mountain junkin' drones.

I'm running late—we'll meet
at the museum. Wait! Her boat is landing
and she can't swim . . .

Breakfast with Flower in Small Vase

      Ranunculus

such a highbrow sound
      for a whorl of yellow plump

but Late Latin for *little frog*

          Persian Buttercup

draft of
      green near the eye
we are
      both sipping our tea

             [ran-the-nun-from-uncle's-oculus!]

        "I am dazzled by your charms"

Imagining the Festival Express
[Riding the Coast Starlight—San Francisco to Seattle]

> *The Grateful Dead, Janis Joplin (with her Full-Tilt Boogie*
> *Band), The Band, Delaney & Bonnie and Friends . . . all*
> *jammed, drank, slept and rode the train in between playing*
> *shows in Toronto, Winnipeg, Saskatoon and Calgary.*
>   *This Day in Music,* 1970

All night a hacking cough in back. Following
the river's snaking shape; screech-steel-clatter

of wheels on tracks also makes a hissing *clackety-*
clack. Chihuahua's bulging eyes in the lap of

the snoring woman I'm assigned to sit beside.
"I don't know where you've been for the last

two days," Joplin crowed to the Calgary crowd,
"but I've been at a party." Snug in the luggage

rack, the ukulele I bought in the Haight I'll learn
to play someday; chunking adds a percussive

sound to your strum. The tour: a bust for the
promoters but Garcia relished the ride. "A train

full of fucking musicians, man, I thought this
was the Orient Express!" Drunk-like walk down

the aisles . . . songs never need to arrive. From
the observation car I watch the sun come up.

Sugared donut hole in a little white box offered
by a gentle hand. Why do I decline? "We

achieved liftoff, for sure," said Weir. Mt. Shasta
rears—so many shaggy-armed pines.

Still Life with Stone

Her obsidian stone grows warm
in my hand; the story she tells of

her father, now passed, who noticed
in his last year new miracles: small

flowers unfurling. The stone makes
no sound but recalls all the rock

grounding us, or the pebble hawk
carried in his mouth, the myth of

how the great mountain came to
be; I sense Santorini's volcanic

black-sand beach hot under my
tanned body before death became

a word I even spoke, before the idea
of holding a stone in your palm to

feel it gather your own fragile heat
could be understood in the open

palm of wanting the fortune teller
to embellish the lines; one dawn

my grandmother simply stopped
breathing; after, the doctor said her

lungs were black—I've told this
story before—she never smoked,

just liked to sit on the back steps
by the driveway watching birds peck

for seeds and grit in the gravel.

for devorah major

Elegy for Chagall
["To My City Vitebsk"]

chickens in the air   over
    j m l
    u b e
            t
              u
                   m
           b
              l
                       e
        f
      o t
     o   o
    r   p   s

blossom-holding
brides-breasts-
bloom

circus   g
under   o
orange   a
orange   t
moon   plays
slice   a violin

purple top-hat man / rabbi green beard six-pointed star

"I didn't have one single painting that didn't breathe
with your spirit and reflection"

16,000 Jews boxed in the ghetto
massacred

he draws
the bow

                   across his
                  yellow-cello
                     body

l   r   s   f   a   t
    o   v   e   l   o

On Dahlias and Mankind

Incomparable flower, tulip lost and found again, allegorical dahlia, it is there, is it not, in this country so calm and dreamy, that we must live and blossom?

Charles Baudelaire

My face thrust over and over into the center of these fire-red petals the fattest bumblebee I have ever seen sucks nectar, plunging, plunging with her tongue. Pollen rubs onto her hairy back legs; a bow moving furiously as if to make phosphorescent music in strains of Yellow! Yellow! Yellow!

Her tibia basket near bursting, I fall ever more into a dream, taken by these eye-altering plants fenced by wrought-iron like exotic animals in a cage.

"Have a nice day!" A man shouts peddling a child's bike on the asphalt around the oval garden."Have a nice day!" he repeats, looping the loop, addressing everyone / no one. "Have a nice day, have a nice . . ."

Innocence in his off-kilter grin; might we all revolve forever in this way? Legs spread wide a painter paints, sweeping strokes, wet on wet, the dazzled ray.

Still Life with Rain

My rain today
—mine, I call it, because
it comes so little here

and don't precious things
make us ache to possess
them more? How to *write*

the sound of tires on a wet
road: a kind of textured
swooshing promises

its own risk. I hear a
crow; his feathers, a glistening
sable I imagine, hold

a haunting undercurrent
but hints of purple luster
invite melancholy, too. I washed

the windows this week, now
the storm washes them again. I
might have waited to see if

the weather report came
true, but I like my view to be
clear, looking out on this dead

end street which once merged
with another named after
a Mexican alcalde of Yerba

Buena murdered by a vigilante
—and yes, a murder is also
a family of crows. I live

alone, with ample time today

to admire Van Gogh's *Wheatfield*
with Crows, in a book borrowed

from the library: a menacing
blue sky, yellow-orange
field, black crows converging

like a great swarm of giant
locusts, and a red path, leading
nowhere . . . intensified

by thick green bands of
grass. One of his last paintings,
the text says, "it signals

his suicide," but to me it's
a manic comfort, the irrefutable
grandeur of the land.

Van Gogh said, "the painter of the future
is a colourist such as there hasn't
been before," in truth describing

himself—as I try between
looking to capture the day; what
do I want from the rain?

On Love & Passion
[*Nude with Calla Lilies*]

> *Perhaps it is expected that I should lament about*
> *how I have suffered living with a man like Diego.*
> *But I do not think the banks of a river suffer because*
> *they let the river flow . . .*
>
> *Frida Kahlo*

She embraces the huge harvest, her long
brown arms like branches reaching
a fountain of flared inflorescence—yellow
spadices rise. We see her from the back, naked
and kneeled, organic as a plant herself,
shadows in orange and green.

The book claims: "perhaps Rivera tried
to apologize to Kahlo with every calla lily
he made—his models as peasant fecundity and
for his pleasure." Of his wife Diego said, "Through
her paintings, she breaks all the taboos of
the woman's body and of female sexuality."

Arrow-shaped leaves emerge from a basket
the length of a large cradle; Kahlo could
not carry their child full term. "I paint
flowers," she wrote, "so they will not die."

Rothko Contemplating Suicide

The reason for my painting large canvases is that I want to be intimate and human.

Of all the images imprisoned within, I want to paint the fields of color, Orange and Tan, which open to warm space like sunflower doors, like reams of light, like folded robes pounded and saffron dyed. *Work of the eye is done,* said Rilke, *now, Go and do heart-work.* The brush is only an extension of the hand, sight a mirror of need, as the huge canvas becomes a burden

to carry but still, to gaze is something more than to mourn; a childhood plagued by czarist troops slaughtering Jews, a Cossack's whip striking my face—these forms to be enveloped within; pools of emotion to plunge into / tragedy, ecstasy, doom / as life flows onto the kitchen floor, thin washes of red, the razor slice a soft-edged opening into the last broad intimacy of something I don't command

Busker with Guitar

Pike Place Market, Seattle

Emancipate yourself from mental slavery
None but ourselves can free our minds.
                              Bob Marley

Plump white peach its juice
dripping from my mouth as I

eat on the crowded cobblestone
street stopped still as always

anywhere by this song, today
beside a mob of peonies so bold

they appear ready to erupt
from their bouquets into riots

of pink redemption. Only ten
bucks for a small bunch but I'm

too broke to buy anything else
and besides such brilliance

seems quickly fated to die. Just
another tourist, I toss a crumpled

buck into the guitar's empty case
as the busker sings: "How long

shall they kill our prophets / While
we stand aside and look?"

Appetites

A guy on Haight shoves a flyer at me. "You know you're hungry!" He hawks. "Hungry!" I glance at the new Indian eatery before waving him off. He repeats (to someone close behind): "you know you're hungry! Hungry!" A few steps more and a different voice in my head . . . luscious French accent and all. Walking in Quebec city, the day before he raced his catamaran back over the Atlantic to St. Malo; how he held my hand—tight like the rigging of a driving sail.

"I'm HUNGRY!" He declared, stopping for a moment on the cobblestones. His body was lean and taut; even his tendons gripped my reserve. "We'll eat," I offered. "No, No, Not zat hungry, ze ozerr hungry!" He tried harder. "*Hangry!*" Seems his crewmate had pissed him off. "Oh . . . you're A-N-G-R-Y," I articulated.

Sex that night was a resplendent storm. The boats embarked near dawn—fit to be tied in the fanfare—he was gone. Now the two words circle in my mind like sharks. HungryAngryHungryAngryHungry. HANGRY! What if we all just fast together for a while and float . . .

Intoxication/Separation/Divorce

Weaving down the street, two drunks
now linger in front of the Salvation Army
where I just left after rummaging—
I had to escape the apartment.

Now, where to linger? A salutation to my armor,
the guys slur something and gesture.
But I had to escape the apartment;
the sun [inside] makes me want to scream.

Blurred eyes: my father would slur something, gesture.
I cross Valencia to the other side.
Their marriage sum: how she wished to scream!
[A Munch face in the throbbing spring.]

I cross Valencia to the other side,
pass an ornamental cherry crazy with blooms.
His morphed face. The throbbing spring;
the new leaves, it seems, are taunting me . . .

pass life like an ornament? Crazy with blooms
I think of the baby egrets near Bolinas Lagoon.
The new leaves [the screams] are taunting me:
"Visit the fledglings! Existence in trees!"

I think. Of the baby egrets near Bolinas Lagoon
parents in the colony take turns. A cycle of wings
visit the fledglings. Existence is free?
This memory might be wrecking me.

Parents in the colony take turns. A cycle of wings—
one nurtures the nest, while the other hunts,

but this memory it is wrenching me:
my mother, weeping, trapped alone in the heat.

Remember: one nurtures the nest, while the other hunts,
but I'm just left with him reeling / rummaging;
my mother weeping—trapped. Alone in the heat
I watch them weaving down the street, two drunks.

The Repair

He might have burned the house
down smoking in the chair. Feet up

on the butler table, the dropped-
down leaf. He'd fumble his lit

cigarette while the stereo would
blare. The theme from *Midnight*

Cowboy once kept Talkin' to the air.
Denver belted out his rocky high for

days without relief. You could hear it
from the neighbor's house; a child

acts unaware. *The Lost Weekend* into
weeks . . . is a bender ever brief?

He'd fumble his lit cigarette, the
scratched-up grooves would blare—

like "Where Is Love" from *Oliver!*
another long drawn out affair. Fagin

I did love though, the Artful
Dodger's faulted chief. Creeping

home [a pickpocket] I was my
father's thief. The song became a

siren, warning he'd be wrecked in
there—feet up on the butler table,

the dropped-down leaf . . . but fine brass
hinges could not bear the weight of

all that grief. I see him now [clamp
and glue] attempting the repair.

The Birds Come Back Each Year

Punk-tattooed tough-looking, my neighbor startles
me standing in my patio when I arrive in the late
afternoon. The black flesh tunnels stretching both
his lobes show the gray sky through them as he

looks up at the eaves under his stairs leading down
here. The blue jay yanked out two of the fledglings
from the nest the juncos return to each year. There's
always this springtime battle between the birds and

they never fail to drag us into it. In his growly smoker's
voice my neighbor assures me he got the babies back
in the nest using my ladder, but he's worried they won't
survive. *I barely touched them but you know, birds*

don't like the scent of human. This is the most I've seen
him in a year, since last April when the birds were at
it again and he kept vigil. He's not aware of how much
I hear of what goes on upstairs. The monthly rows—him

calling his girlfriend *cunt!* and *fucking-bitch!* and her
throwing back full phrases like *the shit that comes out
of your mouth is the same shit that comes out of your
ass* until things, after a while, always go quiet. But

today, in this foggy defused light my neighbor simply
looks sweetly solicitous, and I want to assure him that
it will be all right, that no matter what happens to
the fledglings there will always be next year. I want

to confide that I've left my partner after four years of
love and war; a man who would also hover over baby
birds and yet, we can't save everything I want
to say, though it never hurts [*it hurts*] to try.

Blessing—Rain

The people who weep before my pictures are having
the same religious experience I had when I painted them.
                                                    Mark Rothko

Lunch at Holy Kitchen between teaching
at St. Philip the Apostle School, today's
lesson, paintings after Rothko which

drew a hush from the kids when I described
the emotions he conveyed through fields
of color, how he believed art can unify, make

us more alive—how he decided on suicide:
glasses and shoes removed, the black socks
he wore, arms outstretched, cut where

he bled face-up on the kitchen floor; I am
the lone diner in the restaurant, watching
the rain we haven't received in months; across

24th, a square building, pale blue, with large
picture windows, an orange cat perched
on a tan pedestal staring out of one; I wonder

what cats ponder as they look at rain, creatures
averse to water, do they see silvery streaks,
unattainable minnows swimming? I think

again of the boy in the classroom thrusting
his arm out the open window to feel the rain,
his deep delight at the fresh wet on his

hand, as more water ran down the glass like
transparent paint—the sky a huge gray form
I wished us all to stand before and weep.

3

Star List

Self-Portrait as 13 Responses

after Bahnu Kapil

1.   I am a tree some days. I love earth and birds; becoming rough bark, insect canals, woodpecker braille.

2.   I remember my soft dark body, the moistness within—the quiet sound of rain.

3.   I begin as sky, one cloud stitched at a time. Pinprick of blood smeared over the improvisational patchwork.

4.   I can feel the eucalyptus swaying, the way it enters behind my eyes.

5.   When my limbs are gone, I will swim face first through the sea. I am yellow, iridescent blue.

6.   I come from a great urge to forget. I arrived when the moon was full—I asked for the reflection of light, not the heat itself.

7.   I am my mother who wanted to be a ballerina, starving myself into tutus. Her brother strung her dolls up by their necks hung from the canopy of the poster bed. She sunk her nails into the balsa of his unassembled planes.

8.   Shape is a line which has found its beginning again—my body moves toward the underlying form of the abstraction.

9.   I live now staring into space, asking nothing from the gaze.

10.   Silence is the spirit breathing. *There's a secret in every century that likes it if you shout.*

11.   Death waits in the form of a rickety boat with orchids all around.

12.   If I could I would say everything to everyone without words. For now I'll be the ivy growing over the window.

13.   Today I'm the mute tree as it breathes, its selfish riot of the leaves.

Black

I have dwelt in the blackbird
                                    Guillevic

in the lowering light I watch a lone deer
cross the dry grass, tail

the same black as the crows which keep
calling from far-off trees, columns

                    of black
last night, no stars,
another bad dream
my pupil in the mirror, the bull in the field

the quail's single black head-feather
bobbing near the bush with the black-
striped bees

this poem—black cursive in a black journal

beside me, blackberries
picked along the path

After Separation the Kitchen Fills

After separation the kitchen fills
      with the air of longing; the body
searching for communion with the light
      of what's missing. Is all unattainable?
I am she who waits by the stove warming my hands
      over the blue flame in the absence of you. The iron
      skillet is too heavy to hold; the oil carries me
to olive groves, to the color of your eyes.
There is a heat I cannot bear but will.
We have never met and yet, I hear your voice in the lone crow
      beyond the window
      calling out for the murder where it belongs.

Stepping Beside the Yuba

to walk hard in the bright places.
Charles Wright

a flutter of Anna Blue rise above the slow
                            current flow before collecting again

the heated body of rock knows such waiting
                            is to breathe

a coherent scattering of light on the scales they cling loosely
                            to the wing
                            come off without harm

the river speaks in many forms
                            what we once expressed in gold flecks
                            more scintillating than our field of vision

you said: the swallowtail landing on my arm
                            will always surprise

clouds are snow-capped sierra
                            snow-capped sierra are clouds

Self-Portrait as 10 Responses

after Pablo Neruda

1.   I fall as rain over the city speaking the slang of soot; the spent leaves gesture.

2.   I am a stream moving to avoid salt's sting.

3.   My boat searches for Virgil, who waits for me.

4.   I never wait for anyone. Suffering poses as a bronze statue in patina air.

5.   I am the orange tree dividing my light with the sun.

6.   I am the pink scar of my father's burst appendix.

7.   I arrange my translations with the birds. Everything I say takes flight; I crave the flapping of crows.

8.   The girl inside me plays hide and seek. I'm it—my blindfold slips.

9.   As a tree, I have never learned to talk with the sky, my roots decipher the codex of worms.

10.   All day I stand in the rain; travelers fold smoldering robes into battered trunks of goodbye.

On Love in the Royal BC Museum

where they found
a body drowned
they carved
the shape in stone

how we each are impressed
into the soft mineral
of our love's heart-matter

why must we ever be submerged?

Say instead   spun together
this mass of wool
this whale-bone
spindle whorl

Ritual

the voice of live oaks hides
behind the mask of the raccoon

       rain beats down
       she walks out
       into the calling
       her face risks being
       seen even in the storm

           audible trees

       in concealment
       lies a certain revelation
       even the new moon
       once was a giant yellow
       light they held
       between them

the manzanita's bare want she rearranges
into an altar of glistening bones

Myth

*after a painting of an Aztec Maize
Deity belonging to Frida Kahlo*

In the myth *la diosa* drew
bright pictures of animals
with pigments she collected
from the heat and rain.
Not thinking she had to pay
attention to signs, she buried
her face in shapes   while hands
bent the limbs of the emerging
lay figures into every
awkward angle.

She might have strung
a hammock high up
in the redwoods to rock
the marbled murrelets
to sleep, but she wanted to
remember what it felt like to
write even one love letter before
turning into stone   or how
the shucking of the crickets'
bodies outside the artist's
window in Coyoacán had
at one time made her bleed.

Groves

It was among ferns I learned about eternity.
Robert Bly

Under rock's hood rattlesnake coils; his wet
Trail's dull glisten—the good banana slug.
What would drowned wasps wish from water pails? They
Nearly cut down all the redwoods: *Stumptown.*
Quit when only the final groves stood; their
Girls could pick checker lilies still, hound's tongue.
Should trees bear names of lumber barons? Old
Woodpecker taps out time; chain ferns uncurl.

Forgetting

Armstrong Redwoods State Natural Reserve

Here is your gallery, the strip
of remains, trestles & ties, decks, tables &
chairs: sawmill by Kashaya Falls. Black

birds with beady eyes eat crumbs, greedy
for them. Crow's throated call lower
than the drum of the dry stream

bed. Trees that give off their own dark
rain, hide light from our eyes. *Come back,*
come back down here—trillium, sword

and bracken ferns. Forest theater of bats.
To grow, to be felled, the crash
of 1,400 years. Walking alone, transfixed,

slow-mind sleep. Voles never come down
to the ground, going inward when
they can't speak—envisioning the murrelets

ocean flight each day, everything enveloped
in fog. They dream whatever you died
to remember.

Dusk

the weave
of your ritual basket

breast of moon
thread of dress

the immense trees lie down on the forest floor

acorns' vast tremblings
owl's close moan

even the sound
of far-off things
is ours

Star List

Whitman's perfect silence in the moist night-air

a ship's high guides

a vaudeville show

Saraswati's clear mala beads

the sparkling shawl of the sun

thoughts of the solar system burning

glitter of the cosmos spilled

luminous dots to connect for design

scattered seeds of farmer-angels

sprinkles on midnight ice cream

the coyotes' hunting eyes

the planets playing with pointer lights

makeup Venus wears to go dancing

peepholes in the black curtain of the bright-light stage

a garden of yellow asters in fertile loam

abacus of fate

our night-view ranked the best hotel around

police after they've gone to bed and hung up their jackets sleeping soundly

Stella's own streetcar named desire

Buddha under the bodhi tree tree tree tree tree tree

concave polygons of the great masters

hydrogen and helium having a holiday bash

a poem from a typewriter with just the asterisk key

a *Bateau-Mouche* dinner cruise down the Seine-sky

the fantastic fireworks of calm

seals flecked with silver swimming in the deep

bespangled belly dancers

whirling dervishes transcended

a feast of Purim in the Hebrew sky

Christmas on Canyon Road lit with *farolitos*

a great caravan of camels with candles on their tails

the homes of the seven Rishis granting wisdom

covered wagons moving on the trail of night hung with lanterns

the glint of the giant dipper feeding soup to everyone

Callisto and Arcas safe from Hera's reach

white sheep roaming a black field

silver salmon in the rivers of their birth spawning

a crystal cave

fishermen in canoes lit with oil lamps

silver fish jumping from dark waters

phosphorescent algae in the heavenly ocean

lights left on for you coming home late after the long journey

the sky-country's annual harvest festival

flint from the remarkable fire

the smoldering of coal

a string of lights on the vast patio of night

held together with gas and dust by gravitational attraction

solar system disco ball

Handmade Valentine

Vagina in the center of the heart
is a cut out
      but not cut,
like a calla lily unfolding
yet weeping begonia
          not white.

It's the buckeye sapling's clenched-bud winter,
five palmate spring
      unleashing,
as the planet tickles the waxing,
exquisite above crowd
          laughter.

Memory held, it moves into itself,
moist, swells out
      of itself—
a poppy stop-popping love-orange
or succulent sea
          fruit: yes.

It's the wife's artwork she asks not to share,
a glistening
      in the throb;
the avalanche-quiver of jasmine,
not the dyed feathering
          of words.

It's crow's far chortle in the same chestnut—
here, a grown tree
      with fresh leaves—
a dark bird in the wizened body;
sky-sound in certitude
          of ground.

Photograph

after E.M. Sammis, 1864

I'm riding the ferry to Whidbey Island with
Chief Seattle by my side. He sits on the wall,

a wise old owl, peaked hat on knee, woven
from rush tight enough to hold water carried

from a river with an ancient name no one
remembers. The hat is decorated with a salmon

and a crow, swimming / winging toward each
other and above them stare wide whale eyes. I

imagine were he wearing it, this eloquent elder
would have two sets of eyes to see this sound we

cross, this body of open water not smooth like
the glass he is interred behind and framed only

by the land . . . *there is no death, only a change
of worlds.*

Self-Portrait with Musicians

after the painting, Untitled,
by Gail Tarantino

What we call poetry is the boat.
Robert Duncan

Knees bent, I sit in the middle. One
friend plays a penny whistle, the other
strums a guitar. We are bald: just
the courage of the face unadorned; our

skin tints of purple and green; our small
boat white (a simple bowl) and the sea
a series of white marks too—so our boat
seems to have formed from the water's

gesture. I am the singer, one hand
held near my heart to coax my
voice from there. Blue letters fall
from my mouth into the wide-stroked
waves; they may drift off and form
recognizable words, or not. We can't

shift or move, only hold the ability
to be buoyant in our sound. At night
our boat could be a crescent
moon, the letters cyan
stars. *Listen*: we will never
reach the shore . . .

Self-Portrait as Crow

I am me outside the bathroom
window hidden to her; I
sound my throaty caw
as she washes her face

preparing to write. From her
room she watches as I fly
into sight to land on
the fat wire:

There's a bird that nests
inside you / Sleeping
underneath your skin / When
you open up your wings to
speak / I wish you'd let me in.

I'm me concealed—a user
of tools, I mimic &
steal; the quill I gifted her.

Great Blue Heron Hunts

The sun behind, he was in silhouette
as my hand shielded my eyes. In a shallow
pool on the reef, I saw the step of him
and the flow of his slender neck stretching
forward, curling back as his sharp
sight probed the water for a fish
on which to feed.

With passage from the tide I walked
Bolinas beach. While I did not linger
to witness the elegant shorebird's catch,
I was filled with the moment of him—
stilled by the silent wading of
his lean, long legs—his beak's
indisputable truth.

St. Petersburg [Florida] with Mandelstam

[Dusk]

over the water a shadow
makes the fish hide; how low

can the pelican glide to keep
them awake forever?

[Night]

a heron hunts as the full
moon steps through

the mute bayou. *The people
need poetry that will be their own*

secret.

[Morning]

above palm fronds a bird
conspires balanced

on a wire.

Self-Portrait as the Landscape Painter in Italy

after Jean-Baptiste-Camille Corot

Overwhelmed at first by the light, I
return to these places again and

again, discovering the nuances of
color on the rocks, the trees, the land

—variations of aspect depending on
the time of day. I write home to my

mother: "all I really want to do in life,
is paint landscapes." I adore all my

views, I fall into the terrain's vast
temple: rivers, hills, sky. I rise at

dawn, find vague forms behind a great
white veil: I paint! I paint! Everything

smells sweet until the sun begins to
sear the earth and I see too much. Only

the intangible is splendid—but what is
devotion if not a burning for the divine?

Stepping Beside the Yuba II

the storm seeped water inside
                but the tent held out

thunder louder than the roar of the North Fork below
                but still
                we slept some
the heavy footsteps over us
of neighbors replaced
                by sounds of open space

space above the soaring trees of
                down-lid and drowning stars
        no Venus but a planetary light
        in mind . . .

morning comes with an urgency—
                racket of birds beside
                this deep river pool

green snake moves through water
                as the water
                      between rocks

Stars by Any Other Name

I

       here find Whitman's perfect silence
our lover's inspiration to lie under
fantastic fireworks of intimate calm

we ride the *Bateau-Mouche* late-cruise down
the Seine-sky   Paris is so romantic
our midnight-view room ranked
the best hotel around

II

       the gods' random abacus of how our fates figure
Callisto and Arcas safe from Hera's wrath

fixed locations of enlightenment
flickering figs of the bodhi tree

feast of Purim in the Hebrew dome
the celestial abodes of the seven Rishis' wisdom
Saraswati's clear mala beads gripped in Kali's dark hand

       Venus spilled her glitter

III

       these bespangled belly dancers seduce
       in their raven-silks

       sound-sparks | ebony drum

IV

       salmon scales glimmering up the black river of birth
deep seals flecked silver
phosphorescent algae drifts in the sleep-hour ocean

canoes lit by oil lamps
needlefish jump from murky waters
night-fishermen muse

V

        sables' hunting eyes

        white sheep roaming black fields

            gleam-winged blackbirds

caravan of camels with candles on their tails

VI

        giant dipper glint feeding soup to everyone
queen's jewels given to all
a bag of diamonds tossed by the generous one
gift of luminous pearls

VII

        solar system disco ball
the planets playing with pointer lights

Stella's own streetcar named desire

IX

        grand vigil for existence
matches struck inside the spiral cave

        I type this poem for you
with only the asterisk key **************

NOTES

p. 3   "White" epigraph from "Hangzhou" (tr. George McWhirter).

p. 7   "Virginia Creeper" lyric in italics from "She's Leaving Home," Lennon /McCartney.

p. 14   "The Broken Pitcher, 1891" quote by the artist, William-Adolphe Bouguereau.

p. 27   "Ode to a Jackhammer" lines in italics from Psalm 7:15 (*New International Version*).

p. 30   "April Morning" epigraph from "The Present."

p. 31   "Seeds & Twigs" final line in italics from "Little Song of the Unborn Child," Federico Garcia Lorca (tr. Virginia Barrett).

p. 33   "Breakfast with Flower in Small Vase" final line from http://www.teleflora.com/meaning-of-flowers/ranunculus.

p. 38   "On Dahlias and Mankind" epigraph from "Invitation to the Voyage" (tr. Michael Hamburger).

p. 42   "Rothko Contemplating Suicide" Rilke lines from "Turning Point" (tr. Stephen Mitchell).

p. 43   "Busker with Guitar" epigraph from "Redemption Song." The lines were paraphrased by Marley from a speech by Marcus Garvey delivered in 1938.

p. 53   "Self-Portrait as 13 Responses" in response to Kapil's *The Vertical Interrogation of Strangers* given to me as a writing prompt at a retreat sponsored by *Poets & Writers*; line in italics from "In a House Subcommittee on Electronic Surveillance," Brenda Hillman.

p. 54   "Black" epigraph from "Dwellings" (tr. Denise Levertov).

p. 56   "Stepping Beside the Yuba" epigraph from "Bitter Herbs to Eat, and Dipped in Honey."

p. 60　"Myth" painting referenced is my original work.

p. 61　"Groves" epigraph from "Ferns."

p. 68　"Photograph" final line in italics spoken by Chief Seattle in his oration of 1854.

p. 69　"Self-Portrait with Musicians" epigraph from "A New Poem (for Jack Spicer)." Gail Tarantino is a contemporary San Francisco Bay Area painter.

p. 70　"Self-Portrait as Crow" lyrics in italics from "A Murder of One," Counting Crows.

p. 72　"St. Petersburg [Florida] with Mandelstam" line in italics from Osip Mandelstam's *Selected Poems* (tr. Clarence Brown and W.S. Merwin).

p. 74　"Stepping Beside the Yuba II" line in italics from "Time Is a Graceless Enemy, but Purls as it Comes and Goes," Charles Wright.

Virginia Barrett has published six books of poems and edited two collections of contemporary San Francisco poets. Her work has most recently appeared in the *Writer's Chronicle, Narrative, Roar: Literature and Revolution by Feminist People, Ekphrastic Review, Weaving the Terrain* (Dos Gatos Press), and *Poetry of Resistance: Voices for Social Justice* (University of Arizona Press). She received a 2017 writer's residency grant from the Helene Wurlitzer Foundation of Taos, New Mexico. Her chapbook, *Stars By Any Other Name*, was a semi-finalist for the Frost Place Chapbook Competition sponsored by Bull City Press, 2017. She has been nominated for a Pushcart Prize. She holds an MFA in Writing from the University of San Francisco and an MAT in Teaching Art from the Rhode Island School of Design. She has been a passionate activist and organizer in the San Francisco Bay Area, promoting the arts and education as a path to raising awareness and to building strong communities.

Between Looking, her sixth collection, invites the reader on an excursion into a varied landscape of voice and form. Stylistically, poems range from intimate lyrics to expansive narratives. The work can be playful, meditative, visionary, challenging, and open to experimentation. The thematic span in this collection uses a wide lens. Poems include female-centric pieces on childhood and family history, ekphrastic works exploring issues that artists often face in unsupportive (even hostile) societies, urban-inspired musings, adventures into myth, and mystical encounters in the natural world. What weaves the collection together is a deep need to look out at the world, to gaze as does a painter, to absorb what the eyes see and to offer it back—altered and transfigured in some way.

www.ingramcontent.com/pod-product-compliance
Lightning Source LLC
Chambersburg PA
CBHW021154090426
42740CB00008B/1080